Smell

Judy Wearing

Published by Weigl Publishers Inc.
350 5th Avenue, Suite 3304, PMB 6G
New York, NY 10118-0069
Website: www.weigl.com

Library of Congress Cataloging-in-Publication Data

Wearing, Judy.
 Smell / Judy Wearing.
     p. cm. -- (World of wonder)
 Includes index.
 ISBN 978-1-60596-060-9 (hard cover : alk. paper) -- ISBN 978-1-60596-061-6 (soft cover : alk. paper)
 1. Smell--Juvenile literature. I. Title.
 QP458.W383 2010
 612.8'6--dc22
                              2009008350

Printed in China
1 2 3 4 5 6 7 8 9 0 13 12 11 10 09

j 612.8 WEA 2/26/10 OCLC

Editor: Heather C. Hudak
Design and Layout: Terry Paulhus

All of the Internet URLs given in the book were valid at the time of publication. However, due to the dynamic nature of
the Internet, some addresses may have changed, or sites may have ceased to exist since publication. While the author
and publisher regret any inconvenience this may cause readers, no responsibility for any such changes can be accepted
by either the author or the publisher.

Every reasonable effort has been made to trace ownership and to obtain permission to reprint copyright material. The
publishers would be pleased to have any errors or omissions brought to their attention so that they may be corrected
in subsequent printings.

Weigl acknowledges Getty Images as its primary image supplier for this title.

CONTENTS

What is Smell?

How do you know if perfume smells like fruit or flowers? Your nose tells you so. The scent is made up of tiny **odor particles**. The particles float through the air and into our noses.

Smell is one of our **senses**. It helps us learn about our surroundings.

Almost everyone has a different sense of smell. Only identical twins share this sense.

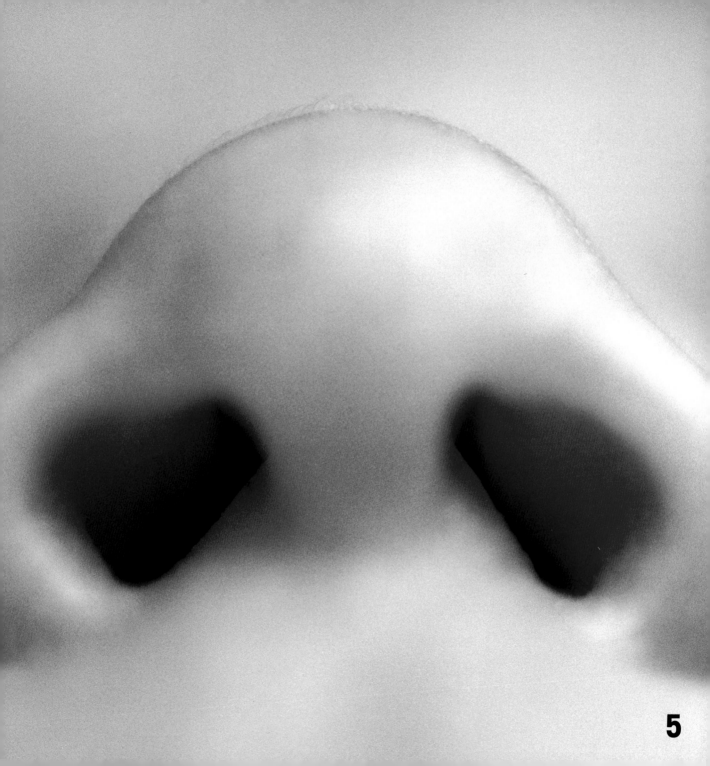

5

Up Your Nose

Have you ever tried to look up a friend's nose? You likely saw many tiny hairs. When odor particles touch these hairs, a message is sent to the brain.

People can smell about 10,000 different odors. Each odor sends a different message to the brain.

The Nose Knows

Did you know some bad smells can warn us of danger? We use natural gas to cook food and heat homes. This gas has no odor. A rotten egg smell is added to it. This helps us tell if there is a gas leak in our homes.

Some animals use scent to mark their **home range**. Grizzly bears rub their body against trees. This warns other animals to stay away.

The animal that smells the worst is the Tasmanian devil.

OFF

LITE ●

LO   HI

1

9

SILVER BAY

9

Happy Smells

Can you think of a smell that makes you happy? If you smell cake, it may bring back happy memories of a birthday party. This is because smells and feelings are connected. Smelling that odor again can change how you feel.

Some smells can make you feel hungry or full. The smell of green apples and mint can make you feel full even when you are not.

Is It Good to Eat?

If you block your nose, can you still **taste** your food? Taste and smell are connected. If you cannot smell your food, you may not be able to taste it very well. A bad smell in the air can make foods taste bad.

Food that smells bad may be rotten. The bad smell is a warning not to eat it.

Smell Power

Did you know sharks can smell their food from one-third of a mile away (536 meters)? Many animals use their sense of smell to find mates, search for food, and avoid **predators**.

Bloodhounds are one million times more sensitive to odor than humans. Police sometimes use dogs called bloodhounds to help them with their work. Their sense of smell is so good that they can find a child who is lost in the woods.

A World Without Odor

How would your life change if you lost your sense of smell? Astronauts in space lose their senses of smell and taste. This is because their noses get stuffed up in space.

Most, but not all, animals can smell. Birds have no sense of smell. They use their eyes and ears to find food and stay safe. Killer whales and dolphins also cannot smell.

When Smell Gets Weak

Did you know that your sense of smell gets stronger as the day goes on? When you wake up in the morning, your sense of smell is weak. The sense of smell also gets weaker as you age. This is why most children can smell better than their parents.

You can lose your sense of smell when you have a cold. A cold can block your nose and stop odors from getting inside.

19

Other Ways of Smelling

How would you know what something smells like if you did not have a nose? Snakes flick out their tongues to smell. Their tongues pick up small pieces of the object they are smelling.

Insects do not have noses, but they still have a very good sense of smell. They use long rods on their heads to smell. These rods are called antennae.

Test Your Sense of Smell

Supplies
three plastic cups, water, lemon juice, orange juice, two spoons, blindfold, large clothes peg or swim clip, tape, and a partner

1. Put a piece of tape on each cup.

2. Write "water" on the first label, "lemon" on the second label, and "orange" on the third.

3. Pour 1/3 cup (79 milliliters) of water in each plastic cup.

4. In the cup labeled lemon, add one spoonful of lemon juice. In the cup labeled orange, add one spoonful of orange juice.

6. Blindfold your partner.

7. Give your partner one spoonful from each of the three cups. Ask your partner to identify the taste—water, lemon, or orange?

8. Have your partner put the clip on his or her nose to block the sense of smell.

9. Give your partner one spoonful from each of the cups in a different order than you did the first time. Ask him or her to identify the taste—water, lemon, or orange?

10. Change places. Now it is your turn to test your sense of smell. Do all the steps again.

11. Compare your results to your partner's results. Did your sense of smell help you taste the lemon and orange flavors? Did you and your partner have the same sense of smell?

Find Out More

To learn more about smell, visit these websites.

Discovery Kids
http://yucky.discovery.com/
flash/body/pg000150.html

Kid's Health
http://kidshealth.org/
kid/htbw/nose.html

Neuroscience for Kids
http://faculty.washington.
edu/chudler/nosek.html

**Children's University
of Manchester**
www.childrensuniversity.
manchester.ac.uk/
interactives/science/
brainandsenses/taste.asp

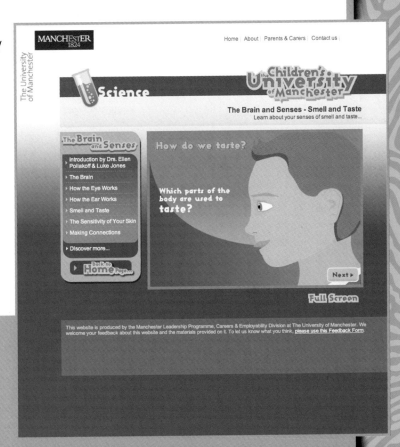

Glossary

home range: the place where an animal lives and hunts

odor: a smell

particles: very small portions of something

predators: animals that hunt other animals for food

senses: the ways the body gets information about what is happening in its surroundings

taste: the sense that provides information about food and other things put into the mouth

Index